Petals of Prayer

Prayers, reflections and resources
for people with dementia, and their carers

Siobhán O'Keeffe

kevin
mayhew

First published in Great Britain in 2011 by Kevin Mayhew Ltd
Buxhall, Stowmarket, Suffolk IP14 3BW
Tel: +44 (0) 1449 737978 Fax: +44 (0) 1449 737834
E-mail: info@kevinmayhewltd.com

www.kevinmayhew.com

ISBN 978 1 84867 329 8
Catalogue No. 1501253

Cover design by Rob Mortonson
© Image copyright Pixelbliss. Used under licence from Shutterstock Inc.
Typeset by Richard Weaver

Printed and bound in Great Britain

Contents

Prayers of general intercession

Resources

Dedication

This book is dedicated with much love and
gratitude to my parents, John and Sheila O'Keeffe.
You blessed my life with compassion and taught me to pray.
May you enjoy eternal life for ever.
Solas na bhflaitheas oraibh.

Acknowledgements

I wish to express my sincere gratitude to my
religious congregation.
Your love, prayer and friendship bless my life each day.

To all whose dementia journey I have the privilege to share,
especially remembering my Auntie Máire, a wonderful inspiration
to me in my support of those with dementia.

To the gentlemen of the Harmony House Early Onset
Dementia Project, Dagenham, I say thank you for your courage,
honesty and great humour. You and your families have
blessed my life in many different ways.

To my colleagues at Harmony House, thank you for welcoming
and supporting our work. We are all on a journey together.

To Eugene Carroll, gifted Dementia Support Volunteer
and friend to us all.

To Fr. Jim McManus, who encouraged me to write
as part of my ministry to those living with dementia.

To David Sheard and Peter Priednieks of Dementia Care Matters
for inspiriational leadership in dementia care.

To my family whose affection and encouragement
have kept my pen flowing over the years.

To Alison, Rebecca and all at Kevin Mayhew, for editorial fine tuning
and warm encouragement of this work. I am indebted to you all.

To you, dear reader, may this work draw us all closer to God and
deepen our understanding of this sacred journey which we share.

About the Author

Siobhán O'Keeffe is a 'Chigwell Sister' born and educated in Cork, Ireland. She is a Registered General Nurse with special interest in palliative care, rehabilitation, health promotion and dementia care. She holds an MA degree in Applied Theology, Justice, Peace and Mission Studies from the Missionary Institute, London. She holds a Diploma in Person Centred Care and is the Co-ordinator of the Harmony House Dementia Support Service in Dagenham, Essex.

Introduction

'Come to me, all you that are weary and are carrying heavy burdens, and I will give you rest.' *(Matthew 11:28).* These words of the Gospel offer comfort to us when we are struggling with an issue that feels bigger than ourselves and greater than our capacity to cope. This may be particularly true when we are caring for a loved one who is affected by dementia. So often we feel utterly helpless and we may feel that we are overwhelmed by fear, confusion and despair. What does the future hold for our loved one and for us? Where can we go for support, comfort and guidance to help us on this new and at times very frightening journey?

We feel so alone, but our compassionate God reminds us that we are never alone. He wishes to offer us the comfort and consolation of his spirit with us and the companionship of others who share a similar journey.

In this series of prayers and reflections I wish to offer you, dear reader, words of encouragement and hope as you travel your dementia journey. You may be a person who has recently received a diagnosis of dementia. You may be the carer, child or friend of a person with this physical disability. Your world may have been changed for ever by what has been happening to you or to the one whom you love. You may feel frightened, lost, alone. You may be struggling to cope with this new mysterious reality; at a loss for words to describe all that is going on for you at this time. You may feel that no one understands or really cares about the anguish of soul that has befallen you. Your peace may be shattered and isolation may be the cross that you bear.

On the other hand, through dementia, you may have discovered a new and deeper sense of yourself or your loved one. Many new blessings may have presented themselves to you. You may be grateful for simple life pleasures and a new, deeper awareness of the gifts in your life. You may have discovered great goodness within yourself or your loved one. The kindness and understanding of friends may have touched you deeply and you may wish to give thanks to God for this manifestation of his love.

You may have new and deeper experiences of God through this sacred journey. You may feel called into an ever-deepening relationship with yourself, your loved one and the God of the journey through this new experience. You may feel that your life of prayer is deepened through this experience and that the Lord is indeed your Shepherd.

You may also need guidance on how to proceed on your journey. You may be thinking: How do I relate to the authorities and care providers? To whom do I go for support? Are there fellow travellers on this journey? Where do I go for help?

In this series of prayers and reflections I have attempted to share some of the experiences of those whose live with dementia and who have shared their journey with me. I do not have dementia, but members of my family are living with this disability. My ministry supporting people living with early onset dementia has touched me deeply and blessed my life. I also observe the lives of older people living with dementia and learn from them. I give thanks to all who have shared their journey with me.

The book starts with a brief overview titled 'What is dementia?' This lists some of the features of different dementias and is not in any way meant to be comprehensive. Each dementia journey is unique and it would not be appropriate to attempt to define scenarios that may or may not happen. A more detailed explanation of Alzheimer's disease is offered in the resources section at the back of the book.

The prayers and reflections are divided into three sections: for those living with dementia, for those caring for someone with dementia, and general intercessions addressing issues of concern to the wider community.

The resources section includes an A–Z of Scripture promises which I hope will be a source of comfort and support to you on your journey. Finally, there are a number of facts and tips. These are just a guideline to what may be available to you. Local services and resources will vary, but national organisations and websites will provide you with helpful information.

May we all grow closer to God together as we travel this sacred journey. May abundant blessing be yours.

Siobhán O'Keeffe

What is dementia?

Dementia is the term used to describe the symptoms of a group of illnesses that cause a progressive decline in a person's functioning. There are a variety of causes.

Dementia can happen to anybody. Most people with dementia are older, but it is important to remember that most older people do not get dementia. It is not a normal part of ageing, but it is more common after the age of 65 years.

The early symptoms of dementia are subtle and may not be immediately obvious. Common symptoms of dementia include:

- progressive and frequent memory loss
- confusion
- personality and behaviour changes
- apathy and withdrawal
- loss of ability to perform everyday tasks.

Types and causes

There are many different types of dementia. The principal ones are:

- *Alzheimer's disease* – this is the most common form of dementia and accounts for between 50 and 70 per cent of all cases. It is a progressive, degenerative illness that attacks the brain.
- *Vascular dementia* – this is the broad term for dementia associated with problems of circulation of blood to the brain.
- *Dementia with Lewy bodies* – abnormal structures called Lewy bodies develop inside nerve cells in the brain.
- *Frontotemporal lobar degeneration (FTLD)* – this is the name given to a group of dementias when there is degeneration in one or both of the frontal or temporal lobes of the brain.
- *Parkinson's disease* – this is a progressive disorder of the central nervous system, characterised by tremors, stiffness in limbs and joints, and speech impediments. Some people with Parkinson's disease may develop dementia in the late stages of the disease.
- *Alcohol-related dementia* – this is caused by too much alcohol, especially with a diet low in vitamin B1 (thiamine). It can be prevented by avoiding alcohol abuse.

- *Aids-related dementia* – is caused by the HIV virus, but does not affect everyone with HIV-Aids.
- *Huntington's disease* – this is an inherited, degenerative brain disease that affects the mind and body. Dementia occurs in the majority of cases.

Diagnosis is important

It is important to confirm a diagnosis of dementia. This will:

- rule out other conditions that can be mistaken for dementia, such as depression, stress, pain or infection
- enable discussion of treatments
- enable planning for the future to start as soon as possible, while the person affected can still actively participate
- allow support to be arranged to assist both the person with dementia and the person's family.

A local doctor or specialist should conduct a full assessment. Your GP should be your first port of call. He or she may make a referral to a Cognitive, Dementia and Memory Service (CDAMS) clinic that can assist in the diagnosis and plan any care.

If the person you are caring for will not go to a doctor or the doctor is unwilling to take your concerns seriously, seek advice on how to deal with these issues from the Alzheimer's Society *(see contact details on p. 110)*.

Prayers and reflections for people living with dementia

Eucharist

Each day, Lord, you invite me to come and celebrate the
Eucharist with you.
To share in your body and blood.
To draw life from your word.
To be fed at the table of life.

I arise,
collect my walking sticks,
leave my home,
cross the road, my husband of 51 years by my side.
We await the bus.
In its own good time it comes. Stops.
We are welcomed aboard by your servant.
We disembark in the city.

Each day I come, Lord, to be with you.
We walk to your altar to take and receive.
'This is my body, this is my blood.'
I hear your words in the core of my being.

Now I know that I am ever more deeply one with you, my God.
My husband of 51 years by my side.
We are fed at the table of the Lamb.
We are ever more deeply one,
one with you, one in you.
Our wellbeing and ever-deepening love is whole in you.
We rejoice and are glad.

We give thanks as our hearts burn within us.
We are one with you. We are one in you.

We continue on our journey.
Lunch in Debenhams.
Home on the bus.
We are all one in you.

Liberty

Do not fear, for I have redeemed you;
I have called you by name, you are mine.
When you pass through the waters, I will be with you;
and through the rivers, they shall not overwhelm you;
when you walk through fire you shall not be burned,
and the flame shall not consume you.
For I am the Lord your God,
the Holy One of Israel, your Saviour.

(Isaiah 43:1–3)

Lord, I thank you that this is your prayer of promise
to all who have dementia.
You are not caught up in labels like Lewy bodies,
vascular dementia, Alzheimer's disease or CJD.
Your vision and compassion move
beyond Government targets and the cost of drugs.
You embrace me with your great compassion
as you reach the core of my spirit
with your liberating, all-powerful words.
I thank you that you wish to liberate me
from the captivity of my fears.
I praise you that you understand
the heartbreaking power of my anxiety
as I fear the loss of my dignity, abilities and social skills.
You understand my pain and isolation
when I struggle to find a word.
You weep with me when I feel shunned by the crowd
and treated as stupid by the authorities.
The oil of your love wipes away the tears of my despair
as I struggle to come to terms with my new reality.
My pain is overwhelming when those entrusted
with my care cannot enter into my bubble.
At times I am trapped in this body which feels alien to me.
A previously simple task becomes an Everest to climb
and I feel so alone.

I sit at your feet and hear your promise of new sight.
Now I see dimly, but with the eyes of my spirit
I see the face of God.
The crowds shout out that I am cursed or even possessed,
yes, I am possessed by you, O Lord.
Gone are the trappings of ego, ambition, success and pride.
I welcome simplicity and childlike faith.

I appreciate the healing touch of a loved one.
A gentle breeze on my face.
The smell of a flower or fresh-baked bread.
The anointing of truth of who I really am in your sight:
a child of God and heir to your kingdom.
The favoured, Spirit-filled, chosen of God.
Child of the new Jerusalem.
Birthed in the risen Christ.
Whole, integrated and one in you.

Free,
Spirit-filled,
blessed and chosen;
a new creation.
Blessed and deeply at peace,
grateful.

As for you, my cross has become my resurrection.
I am birthed in the Risen Christ and I am free.

Emmaus

As they came near the village to which they were going, he walked ahead as if he were going on. But they urged him strongly, saying, 'Stay with us, because it is almost evening and the day is now nearly over.' So he went in to stay with them. When he was at the table with them, he took bread, blessed and broke it, and gave it to them. Then their eyes were opened, and they recognised him.

(Luke 24:28–31)

Yes, Lord, my eyes have been opened.
My body has been broken in the journey into dementia.
Spirit stripped bare.
Stripped bare of all illusion, all pretence.
The cloak of success, independence, pride have fallen away.
I stand naked before you.

In return you look on me with great eyes of love.

You offer me your hand:
'Take and eat, this is my body broken for you.
Take and drink, this is my blood poured out for you.
Food for the journey,
a journey of union.
You are called ever more deeply into me.
I am the source of all power, the fountain of life,
living water, healing spring.
You have been washed clean in my blood.'

My eyes have been opened,
opened wider to your love.

Purple coat

Today Lord, I saw it,
my purple coat.
The coat of my dreams.
Young again.
The carefree girl I have always been.
Young at heart.
Ninety years of life,
I never grow old.
Always alive in you.
This purple coat fitted just right.
Perfect!
Pure joy!
I felt a million dollars.
A credit crunch cannot bite my spirit
I felt like a queen!

Then I remembered, Lord, you too had a purple coat;
they dressed you up in purple,
twisted some thorns into a crown and placed it on your head.
And they began saluting you, 'Hail, King of the Jews!'
They struck your head with a reed and spat on you,
and they went down on their knees to do you homage.
And when they had finished making fun of you,
they took off the purple and dressed you in your own clothes.[1]

I felt wrapped in your love as I wore my purple coat;
yours was the coat of saving love.

As I wear my coat I see its buttons of beauty,
its hem of security,
the belt of integrity,
the robe of justice,
the collar of truth
because of your coat of saving love.

1. Adapted from Mark 15:16–20

Food and drink

These all look to you to give them their food in due season;
when you give to them, they gather it up;
when you open your hand, they are filled with good things.
(Psalm 104:27, 28)

Today our meals were placed before us.
This was an experience of grace for us.
Food that we might like to eat had been carefully chosen.
Shopping, cooking and serving invited us to eat.
A beautiful presentation of your gift of food
encouraged us to gather around a table;
our senses came to life at the colours before us,
rich smells invited us to partake in life-giving food.
People chosen to share our journey
helped us to choose what we might enjoy.
They sat beside us and gently supported us in our choice
of food and your gift of drink.
They did not rush us but delighted in our joy as we partook of
each morsel on our plate or sipped from the glass before us.
A few chosen companions decorated our table
with cloths, candles and flowers.
The individuality of each one was respected
as their favourite cup, mug or plate
was placed where they like to dine.
Our celebration opened with a song of thanksgiving
for food, drink and all your gifts to us.
We gave thanks for all who support us and remembered those
who do not have enough to eat.
Deep in our hearts we prayed that the resources of your world,
O Lord, be equally shared so that none go hungry
while barns overflow with life-giving food.
'From your lofty abode you water the mountains;
You cause the grass to grow for the cattle,
and plants for people to use, to bring forth food from the earth,
and wine to gladden the human heart, oil to make the face shine,
and bread to strengthen the human heart.[2]

2. Adapted from Psalm 104:13–16

Trusting in God's infinite care

The Lord works vindication and justice for all who are oppressed.
(Psalm 103:6)

Lord, I come to you in all my need.
I feel so oppressed as I have had
more than my share of scorn,
more than my share of jeers from the complacent,
of contempt from the proud.

I feel that many of your people look at me and laugh;
they deride me for my seeming lack of understanding;
they say that I do not have a voice.

In their arrogance they pass me by
and do not attempt to engage with me;
in their ignorance they lack the insight to know
that I feel and sense all that is going on around me.

My lips may have fallen silent
but my heart is more fully alive than ever before.
I know who cares for my wellbeing and who scorns
the life in my being.

This toxic attitude could stifle my spirit
but I keep my mind and heart fixed on you.
I trust that one day the scales may fall from their eyes and hearts
when we may all celebrate our oneness in you.

'Hope in God; for I shall again praise him,
my help and my God.'[3]

3. Psalm 42:5, 6

Healing

'Your faith has made you well; go in peace, and be healed of your disease.'

(Mark 5:34)

Christ, you invite us to pray with great faith and confidence
for all who suffer any disability or illness.
You wish to bestow your gift of peace on all.

Disability, brokenness, memory loss,
confusion, communication difficulties, challenging behaviours,
disorientation, fragility:
these do not exclude anyone
from the unconditional promises of God.
He reminds us, 'Do not fear, only believe.'[4]

His desire is to restore all to good health as he commands us
to 'stretch out our hand' so that it may be made better.[5]

He will take us by our hand and help us up
so that our illnesses of fear and other things may leave us
and we may serve him and all of God's people.[6]

We will return to our homes and
'declare how much God has done for us'.[7]
We will recognise Christ ever more deeply
as the 'Holy One of God'.[8]

Our prayer of gratitude will be
'He has done everything well'[9]
and we will cry out, 'to the One seated on the throne
and to the Lamb
be blessing and honour and glory and might
for ever and ever!'[10]

4. Mark 5:36
5. Mark 3:5
6. based on Luke 4:38, 39
7. Luke 8:39
8. Mark 1:24
9. Mark 7:37
10. Revelation 5:13

Songs of praise

O Lord, in the morning you hear my voice:
in the morning I plead my case to you, and watch.
(Psalm 5:3)

We, the people who live with dementia,
our loved ones, carers, advocates and friends
cry out with joy before the living God.

We bow down and worship you, O God, in gratitude for all who love and support us on our journey.

We give thanks for progress made in medical research
trusting that, one day soon,
oh so soon, a cure will be found;
a gene identified, a healing drug delivered
with loving sensitivity to us all.
We pray that misunderstanding
will give way to compassionate embrace.
As one body we will grow in loving understanding
of you and each other.
May we all be one in you.
You redeemed your people by your precious blood.
Come, we implore you, to our aid.
Grant us with the saints a place in eternal glory.
Lord, save your people and bless your inheritance.
Rule them and uphold them for ever and ever.
Day by day we praise you,
we acclaim you now and to all eternity.
Cure or no cure, O God, we your people will always praise you.
We ask that in your goodness, Lord,
you keep us free from sin;
have mercy on us, Lord, have mercy.
May your mercy always be with us, Lord,
for we have hoped in you.
We praise you, O God, and we acclaim you as our Lord.
Blest be your holy and all-powerful name,
Amen, Amen, Amen.

Fired at 45

Out of the depths I cry to you, O Lord.
Lord, hear my voice!
Let your ears be attentive
to the voice of my supplications!
(Psalm 130:1, 2)

Lord, I was fired from my job today!
Dismissed without warning!

My boss said that I was 'incompetent,
performing poorly and not meeting company targets'.
He went on to say that I had 'lost my ability to be a team player'
and that I did not fit into the professional
or social structure of the organisation.
There was no place in the office for someone who lacked
good organisational and social skills
and I would be better suited to an alternative career.
The interview had ended before
I could comprehend what was happening to me.
My world was falling apart with each word that I heard.
This could not possibly be happening to me!
I served this company faithfully for 20 years
and I am only 45 years old.
Consigned to the scrap heap. Dismissed. Cast aside.

Where does this leave me now?
My wife and children depend on me to place food on the table.
My children's shoes need to be replaced every few months.
The mortgage agreement does not end for another 10 years.
What will happen to my pension rights? Care in old age?
Who will pay for my daughter's wedding?
I remember my own wedding day so well.
A day of such deep, deep joy!

I am 45 years old.
Lord, I am completely and utterly shattered.
This nightmare has crushed my soul.

Yes, I have grappled with word-finding problems for some time now;
I cannot follow directions in the clear, crisp way
that I have always known.
Sometimes getting dressed is a struggle.
I put shoes on the wrong feet.
A jumper appears upside down.
Buttons and zips, an impossible task.
Colour co-ordination, a living nightmare.
My moods are erratic for no known reason;
I weep at the most unexpected and inappropriate times;
arguments with those I love happen without warning.
I feel so broken, so frightened, so alone.

But in the midst of my grief I hear you say to me:

If God is for us, who is against us? He who did not withhold his own Son, but gave him up for all of us, will he not with him also give us everything else? Who will bring any charge against God's elect? It is God who justifies. Who is to condemn? It is Christ Jesus, who died, yes, who was raised, who is at the right hand of God, who indeed intercedes for us. Who will separate us from the love of Christ? Will hardship, or distress, or persecution, or famine, or nakedness, or peril, or sword? As it is written,

> 'For your sake we are being killed all day long;
> we are accounted as sheep to be slaughtered.'

No, in all these things we are more than conquerors through him who loved us. For I am convinced that neither death, nor life, nor angels, nor rulers, nor things present, nor things to come, nor powers, nor height, nor depth, nor anything else in all creation, will be able to separate us from the love of God in Christ Jesus our Lord.

(Romans 8:31–39)

Your words, O Lord, seep through my being and I am at peace.
Fired at 45 but resting in your unconditional love for me.
At peace. Deeply at peace.

Sit at my feet

He entered a certain village, where a woman named Martha welcomed him into her home. She had a sister named Mary, who sat at the Lord's feet and listened to what he was saying.

(Luke 10:38, 39)

Lord, I thank you for the very special gift
that you offer to all who live with dementia.
You come to me and you seek out a home where you may rest.
You have journeyed far and wide sharing a message
of redemption, healing and new life.

Now you need to rest and be with your closest friends.
In your divinity you wish to live out your humanity and rest.
You acknowledge your need for deep companionship
and you are hungry.
You wish to come home to a place of safety
where you will be accepted for who you are.
A place free from questions, expectations and threats.

You come to me as I live with dementia.
You seek me out because with me your spirit rests in a new way.
You speak to me at the deepest level of my being
and remind me of my great dignity.
You recognise that I desire to be with you;
this is the deepest desire of my heart and a free gift from you.

You know that I live in a society
that does not always understand my disability
or recognise who you are.
You know that I recognise you in the breaking of bread.
I love you with the deepest level of my being
and you see and feel and touch that great love.

In your infinite compassion you wish to share
your great love with me and I am so grateful.
My mind, attention and heart are totally focused on you.
You are the joy of my heart,
the hope of my spirit and the reason for my being.

Unlike Martha, I am not distracted with all the serving
because I am not as able to do these tasks as before.
I have become more dependent on my fellow human beings
for my survival, but I have been enriched
by a deeper knowledge of you.
I am able to sit at your feet and listen.
I listen with undivided attention,
without prejudice or fear, because I know who you are.
You accept me with unconditional love and I thank you.
The longer I sit at your feet and listen,
the more I learn of you; meek and humble of heart.
The more time I spend in your gracious presence,
the more I desire you.
You draw me ever more deeply into your love
and I am deeply at peace.
I have come home to who I really am and my joy is complete.

I recognise that this new knowledge of you
is a fruit of my dementia.
I have suffered greatly on my journey
as I have grappled with loss, grief, misunderstanding and pain
but now I know a new and deeper peace.

This gift of your peace is free of charge and there for receiving
if I can be still and sit at your feet and listen.

I thank you that the gentle service of my loved ones,
who become Martha for me,
frees me to sit at your feet and listen.
They too hear your voice in a different way and respond in love.
Bless them with your love, Lord,
touch them with my gratitude.
Deepen their knowledge of you.
May I be a channel of light to them
so that we may in ever new ways sit at your feet and listen.
May we always choose the better part,
may it never be taken from us.
As Trinity may we sit before you
and listen in love to the one who is love.

The allotment

Lord, we wish to thank you for our beautiful allotment.
We have been gifted by you with this green space where
we gather with our friends,
till the soil,
plant little seeds,
water the ground,
relax in the sunshine and
be one with all creation.

This is a place of healing and peace for us.
We touch the earth,
feel its soft moisture between our fingers,
chat,
reminisce about earlier years
when we cared for our gardens
and grew food for our loved ones.
The mysterious word, 'dementia',
is never mentioned at the allotment.
We gather in our full humanity to work
and enjoy the beauty of your creation.
Birdsong fills the air and a gentle breeze brushes our cheek.

The allotment is a place of beauty and safety
for many who share your cross,
some struggling with fragile mental health;
those at risk of social isolation because of age or infirmity
are welcome.
We drink tea together and rest in your love.
All is your gift to us and free of charge.

As we work we are reminded to be gentle with the soil
as we remove the weeds
that have threatened to choke the new seed;
we wish to have a 'perfect patch', the neatest in our borough,
to lead pure and spotless lives before you;

in our desire to be perfect as you are perfect
we wish to remove anything that does not look or feel right
in the soil of our lives.

As you know, Lord, we who live with a dementia
are highly sensitive and desire great beauty.
You graciously remind us not to pull out the weeds,
'for in gathering the weeds
you would uproot the wheat along with them.
Let both of them grow together until the harvest;
and at harvest time I will tell the reapers,
"Collect the weeds first and bind them in bundles to be burned,
but gather the wheat into my barn."'[11]

Lord, we thank you for your patience with us.
We thank you that you accept us as we are,
rather than as we feel we should be.
We thank you that you offer us a lifetime of growth
to become who you desire us to be.
We thank you that you offer us this beautiful space
where we are able to pray and reflect on your word.
We thank you that our disability does not block us
from hearing your voice
but that through it we hear you in ever new ways.
May we hear your word, share your word
and live by your word in ever new ways.
We bless you, Lord and creator of all, Amen.

11. Matthew 13:29, 30

Knitting

'It was you who formed my inward parts;
you knit me together in my mother's womb.
I praise you, for I am fearfully and wonderfully made.
Wonderful are your works; that I know very well.'
(Psalm 139:13, 14)

Lord, I marvel at the story of my life.
You created me in love
and carried me through each moment of each day.
You remind me that your plan for my life has always been good,
and now more than ever you call me to trust this all-loving plan.
You remind me of the words you spoke to your prophet Jeremiah:
'I know the plans I have for you, for your welfare and not for harm.'[12]
I know, Lord, that this all-loving plan has not changed
despite my newly diagnosed dementia.

I am 50 years old.

The mystery of life broke forth before me in a new way today, Lord.
The simple act of picking up my knitting needles
unleashed a flood of memories.
A set of stitches will unfold into a baby bonnet.
My daughter is 25 years old and 'is with her first child' .
She is soon to give birth.
Excitement wells up in our beings at the thought of
the new life growing deep within her womb.
Wonderful memories of my own pregnancy with her 25 years ago
flood back and I am filled with deep, deep joy.

Maria has blessed her father's and my life in so many ways
and we are so grateful to her.
She has always been kind to me, but especially since
I began to lose my memory just a little while ago.
I failed to notice that I was not well when I went to Tesco
one day and filled my trolley with 22 loaves of bread.

12. Jeremiah 29:11

Only my husband, Joe, and I live at home now,
our children have moved out but are always in our hearts.
Why would we need 22 loaves of bread?
I wrote a shopping list before I went shopping
but could not understand it as I walked around the store.
More and more goods were displayed on the shelves
and I did not know where to turn.
Music and advertisements assaulted my senses on every aisle
and I felt lost and frightened.
The friendly shopkeeper whom I had known when I was younger
was nowhere to be seen.
I did not know what to do and I felt confused.

Then I remembered that I needed to buy bread.
The lovely aroma of freshly baked bread
drew me to the bread counter and I felt safe.
I started to fill the trolley with loaf after loaf after loaf.
I was back in control and the tears that had been welling up
in my eyes began to drift away.
Loaf after loaf after loaf appeared in my trolley
and my breathing regained its normal relaxed rhythm.

When I went to the checkout I got some strange looks
and heard unkind comments from fellow shoppers.
'What is she going to do with all that bread?'
I was unable to pay and started to cry.
I felt dreadful and just wanted to go home.

The young girl asked me if I had any family at home.
I told her that my husband, Joe, was at work
and could not be disturbed.
I told her of my daughter, Maria,
and said that she would be at home preparing the dinner.
I even told her about the beautiful new baby
that she is expecting any day now.
The young girl – I don't remember her name – rang Maria
and asked her to come and take me home
as I 'appeared a little confused and upset'.
I was taken into a little office and given a cup of tea.

This nice young girl sat with me
and told me that everything would be OK.
I remembered hearing you say that
'Pleasant words are like a honeycomb,
sweetness to the soul and health to the body.'[13]

Maria arrived, smiled, and I immediately felt safe.
My new friend told her what had happened
and Maria gently led me to her car.
I had forgotten that she has a car.
I remember her learning to ride her bicycle
and now she has a lovely pink car.
How times have changed!
She drove me to my home.
Oh to be back indoors!
Everything is familiar here,
no blaring radio, crowds or pressure to buy.

Maria encouraged me to see our family doctor –
we believe in your gift of doctors –
and we went together to see a man
who has been our lifelong friend.
I knew that I needed help and felt that it is important to
have faith in those whom the Lord has blessed
with a healing ministry.

'"In the name of Jesus Christ of Nazareth, stand up and walk."
And he took him by the right hand and raised him up;
and immediately his feet and ankles were made strong.'[14]

The doctor referred me to the Memory Service for assessment
and I was given the devastating news that I had dementia.
I just felt bewildered.
This was not something that younger people experience
or so I thought.

Staff were kind.
They told me of the importance of keeping busy,
doing the things that I enjoy
and spending time with my loved ones.

13. Proverbs 16:24
14. Acts 3:6–8

They asked me if I had any hobbies or particular interests
that brought me great pleasure.
I immediately told them of my passion for knitting
and of the new life
that was blessing our family in the coming weeks.
With each word that I spoke I felt better.
The doctor and the psychologist reminded me of
the importance of keeping up knitting
and of not becoming too tired.
Today, Lord, I will just do a few more rows of
the little bonnet and I will rest.
I will use this new way of living with my disability
to pray for all expectant mothers.
The little ones that they carry are known by you
through and through;
you watch their bones take shape
while they are being formed in secret,
knitted in the limbo of the womb.[15]

Like Mary your mother, may they rejoice and cry out,
'Let it be with me according to your word.'[16]

Like Elizabeth, may we the people who journey with them
recognise the blessing of each life and give you undying thanks.

I pray also for all mothers whose children die before their birth;
for those who are traumatised in delivery
or at any point of their life journey.
I pray with Elizabeth, who knew the pain of barrenness,
for all who are unable to conceive or bring safely to birth.
I pray for parents whose children have pierced their souls
with a lance or who no longer know you
as Lord of their lives,
all who never say, 'Truly this man was God's Son!'[17]

Knit us all together again by the power of your love. Amen.

15. Adapted from Psalm 139:15
16. Luke 1:38
17. Matthew 27:54

Seashells

The heavens are telling the glory of God;
and the firmament proclaims his handiwork.
(Psalm 19:1)

Oh Lord, I love the sea.
Its majesty, power and beauty fill my soul.
It draws me to its shores every weekend;
I stand on the shore in awe before you.

My wife and I love to get away
to our caravan on Friday evening.
This is our place of refuge
far from the din of the city as the sun goes down.
Mersea Island has been our sanctuary for many years;
this is a place of healing and peace for us.
We give you thanks for the roads that lead us
to you in this hallowed place.

The pressures of everyday living with dementia
float away in the sea.
Beautiful seashells are washed ashore;
I fall on my hunkers and collect seashells,
big shells,
small shells,
white shells,
brown shells,
blue shells,
every colour shell,
every shape shell,
every beautiful shell
that floats before me.

I fall on my knees and give you thanks,
Creator of all beauty.

Shell craft has become one of my day centre pleasures.
A beautiful shell mosaic is taking shape at my hands,
a gift for my faithful wife of 40 years,
the lady who walks beside me on this new,
mysterious,
at times frightening,
confusing
lonely journey.

She is a lady of integrity,
wisdom,
commitment,
deep love.

Her beauty and mystery unfold in new ways
every passing year.
I give you thanks, O my God,
for all that she means to me.

Delicate shell work also challenges me;
my skills are not what they once were.
I sometimes forget how to glue a shell into the mosaic.
My friends support me with gentleness and care.

At home I await an occupational therapy assessment.
My daily living skills are slipping a little:
washing, dressing, sandwich-making . . .
you know the rest, Lord.

Down by the seashore, I forget all:
my heart, my mind, all my senses are focused on you.
I give you thanks for the beauty of the sea,
I give you thanks for the beauty of seashells,
I give you thanks for my beautiful wife,
I give you thanks for all of life.
I know, Lord, that your love for me is as constant
as the grains of sand on the shores of the sea.

Death of my dog

Blessed are those who mourn, for they will be comforted.
(Matthew 4:4)

My dog died today.
He became ill suddenly.
We took him to the vet;
he was put to sleep.

Lord, I feel so lost without my beautiful friend.
He was always so loyal to me.
We went to walk in the park and met many lovely people.
Many had their dogs with them.
We paused and shared a moment of beauty together.
Now he is gone and I don't know what I will do.

My beautiful dog reduced my sense of isolation
when I began to have problems with my memory and other things.
My job became too difficult for me.
The door on my paid working life closed and I felt so alone.

I have a wonderful wife.
She cares for my every need
but she has to go to work each day, Lord.
You know how it is –
bills to be paid, food to be placed on the table,
treats for our grandchildren.
I feel bad that I am not able to help her more,
but you know the limitations my dementia places upon me.

I am at home, alone, three days a week.
My friend comes and cares for me two days a week.
But my beautiful dog was my companion seven days a week.
There was no charge for 24/7 care.
Now, my dog has gone.
I feel so alone.
I have wept and wept and wept today, Lord.

The wuff, wuff has fallen silent;
the gentle paw on my lap will be no more;
my heart breaks within me.

Please touch my soul, Lord, with words of comfort and hope.

The scriptures tell us that you, Jesus,
wept over the death of your friend Lazarus [18]
and that you cried out and asked to be taken to see him.

I know, Lord, that there is no comparison
between the grief that I feel today and
the grief you felt when Lazarus died;
but my pain today, Lord, is real and
I need your touch.

In the silence you gently remind me
that you will transform this pain for me,
you will be glorified through it.
Ministers of healing grace will be sent to me.
These ministers are my day centre friends.
I can talk so honestly and openly
with the other men about all that is going on in my life.
We are real with each other,
each carrying his own heartaches
but also a great deal of joy.
It is so good to be human together.
You know, Lord, they all have dogs!

I think animals help us to be more human;
they bring out the compassion that you
have placed within our spirits
to care for all your creation.
They bond us together,
they draw us out of ourselves,
they forgive us without question when we get it wrong.
There is no judgement, no resentment, no bitterness.
They never exclude us because of our dementia,
They call all your people to be ever more human.
To touch the divine.
They are indeed our friends.
We pray, Lord, for the protection of all your creatures.

18. John 11:35

May we recognise them as your gift to us.
May we treat them with gentleness,
kindness and the respect that is their due.
We thank you for the many ways in which they
draw us ever closer to each other and to you.
May we all bless and praise you with one voice, for ever. Amen.

Tulip Café

Tulip Café,
place of safety,
in the middle of town,
walking distance from my home.
Refuge from loneliness,
centre of friendship;
tea freshly brewed,
one cup in every seven free of charge,
Tulip Café,
balm for my soul.

People need people.
You said of Adam,
'It is not good that the man should be alone.'[19]
Friends share a smile,
waiters who have you as their model
in Tulip Café;
waitresses who listen with hearts that understand,
hearts that do not judge,
hearts that free me to be who I am,
share a cup of 70p tea
in Tulip Café.

Here is my servant, whom I uphold,
my chosen, in whom my soul delights;
I have put my spirit upon him;
he will bring forth justice to the nations.
(Isaiah 42:1–2)

19. Genesis 2:18

Kitchen porter

Lord, I thank you for all who supported me in my little job today.

The gentleman who works as the kitchen porter at the
dementia day centre is on holiday this week.

I have been asked if I would like to help out in the kitchen.

I rejoiced at the opportunity to work.

For so long now I have been unable to work.
I have felt frustrated, useless, lost;
a new opportunity presented itself and I gave thanks.

This work was new to me;
I had never worked as a kitchen porter before.
Clearing tables, washing dishes,
scrubbing large industrial saucepans –
it was good to feel the energy of work flow through my bones.

People were kind;
they listened,
showed me what to do,
remembered that I have problems following instructions.
They were patient;
they did not make me feel diminished,
but built up my self-esteem.
My confidence and sense of self-worth
grew with each passing hour.
I was at peace among friends,
we were all one.

Alzheimer's disease has brought me new friends.
I give you thanks,
I bless you, Lord,
for the gift of a little work.

I pray for all who, because of dementia,
are no longer able to work.
Bless them with courage, grace and good friends.

'Whoever wishes to be first among you must be slave of all.
For the Son of Man came not to be served but to serve,
and to give his life as a ransom for many.'

(Mark 10:44, 45)

Trip to the zoo

God said, 'Let the earth bring forth living creatures of every kind: cattle and creeping things and wild animals of the earth of every kind.' And it was so. God made the wild animals of the earth of every kind, and the cattle of every kind, and everything that creeps upon the ground of every kind. And God saw that it was good.

(Genesis 1:24, 25)

You blessed us, Lord, with a beautiful day today.
We thank you.
You invited us to take a trip to the zoo!

We are a little group,
three good friends,
living with dementia.
We met at a day centre
and enjoy each other's company.

Our love of nature is recognised by family,
friends and support workers.
A trip to the zoo felt right.
One of our number offered us
Tesco Club Points to pay our entrance fee;
generosity is your gift to us,
we thank you.

We travelled by car.
A trip on the London Underground was not possible:
the spirit of one of our friends has been deeply wounded
by the London bombing, 7/7
– he now fears travelling underground.
Father, forgive them!

The beauty of your creation was everywhere to be found.
We thank you,
We bless you,
We praise you.

A picnic lunch,
crumbs shared with the birds who sat at our table,
chips and ice cream,
sunshine,
warmth,
friendship,
love;

we were reminded of your words:

'God saw everything that he had made,
and indeed, it was very good.'
(Genesis 1:31)

Hens and chickens

Good morning, Lord.
Today I wish to give thanks for beautiful,
gentle hens and their little chicks.

These little creatures have brought such joy into my life.
They provide me with a little job;
I am so happy to be able to care for them.
I gather food for them each day.
I leave my home to go to their little house.
I feed them and give them water.

I ensure that their home is secure –
'Foxes not welcome' is the invisible sign over the door!

You have gifted hens with an ability to provide us with food,
fresh eggs for breakfast,
eggs for baking and for lemon meringue pie –
oh, the delight of an egg!

I gather the eggs,
take them home and share them with my family.
A little egg, a brown egg,
a white egg, a little speckled egg –
oh, the delight of an egg!

Lord, you know that I have memory problems,
but I never forget to care for my hens.
They are precious to you and precious to me.
I am reminded, Lord, of your care for all of your people;
we are all precious to you.
You cry out, 'How often have I desired
to gather your children together
as a hen gathers her brood under her wings,
and you were not willing!'[20]

20. Luke 13:34

You beseech us, Lord, to listen to your voice,
to walk in your ways,
to experience your fullness of life;
'I came that they may have life, and have it abundantly.'
(John 10:10)

Like the shell of an egg, may our hearts be broken open
to receive your life-giving word;
may the yoke of your goodness flow through our lives,
may we be bearers of your new life wherever you ask us to be.

Oh, the delight of an egg!

Trinity

'Where two or three are gathered in my name,
I am there among them.'
(Matthew 18:20)

Our dementia group has three members,
three 'gentle' men.
Trinity.

The presence of your sons among us blesses us.
We feel you walk with us,
we hear you talk with us,
we know you listen to us,
are ever present with us.

A little group, so small,
challenges those who hold the key to project funding.
So much today is number- and target-driven.
This is not how you view the world, Lord;
people are your concern;
your suffering, poor ones are closest to your heart.

Your presence blesses us ever more deeply than silver or gold.
Love is the key to the safe of your heart.
We know that you will continue to bless your children,
bestow on us all that we need;
you will pour forth your blessings on your children.
Bless the Trinity among us.

May the Trinity of Father, Son and Spirit be ever among us,
Amen, Amen, Amen.

Vince

I will sing of your might;
I will sing aloud of your steadfast love in the morning.
(Psalm 59:16)

We thank you, Lord, for your servant Vince.
He is gifted with a generous heart and a gentle voice.
Vince comes to our group of new life and leads us in song.

We hear your words deep within our hearts:

'Blessed are you, O Lord, the God of our ancestor Israel,
for ever and ever.
Yours, O Lord, are the greatness, the power, the glory,
the victory, and the majesty;
for all that is in the heavens and on the earth is yours;
yours is the kingdom, O Lord,
and you are exalted as head above all.
Riches and honour come from you, and you rule over all.
In your hand are power and might;
and it is in your hand to make great and to give strength to all.
And now, our God,
we give thanks to you and praise your glorious name.'
(1 Chronicles 29:10–13)

We respond in love.

We sing in full voice the songs we have loved
throughout our lives.
Words flood back, happy memories are rekindled;
we savour the presence of one another,
we grow to know each other better;
bonds of friendship are deepened
within a group of friends
which has been born through our dementia.
We give thanks for each other;
we are at peace.

Fruit picking

For everything there is a season,
and a time for every matter under heaven:
a time for planting,
a time to pluck up what has been planted.
(Ecclesiastes 3:1, 2)

We gathered together yesterday
to pick beautiful new fruit and vegetables:
strawberries, tomatoes, redcurrants, blackcurrants;
gifts of your earth.

In a few short weeks, tiny seeds and little plants
had burst forth into new life.
Glorious sunshine, regular watering
and the removal of life-draining suckers
had called forth the new life that lay within the seed.
In the depths of the soil, hope was bursting forth,
the time of harvest had come.

This was a day of celebration for us,
a moment of unity and oneness.
We helped each other as we gathered the produce of the earth.
Fruit was gently gathered taken and shared,
chatter and laughter filled the air –
nothing was said about dementia.

We did what we had always done at this time of the year:
we reaped beautiful fruit and we gave thanks.
We were deeply at peace beneath the rays of your sunshine,
in the company of our friends.
We remembered and prayed your words:
'When a worker finds happiness in work, this is a gift from God.'[21]

Gather us, O Lord, as one before you,
may the fruit of your word, deep within the soil of our hearts,
burst forth into new life.

21. Adapted from Ecclesiastes 3:12

'The good person
out of the good treasure of the heart
produces good,
and the evil person
out of evil treasure produces evil;
for it is out of the abundance of the heart
that the mouth speaks.'

(Luke 6:45)

May we be a blessing to your people here on earth;
may the warmth of your love melt away anything that is not of you;
may the broken and vulnerable find rest in our presence;
may we bear a harvest of kind words
and good deeds for your kingdom;
may we meet in the barn of eternal life;
may we sing out your praise for ever and ever. Amen.

Crossing the road

Jesus went about all the cities and villages, teaching in their synagogues, and proclaiming the good news of the kingdom, and curing every disease and every sickness.

(Matthew 9:35)

Lord, I ask that you bless and protect me as I cross the road.
Bless my coming and going.
Please protect me in the confusion that surrounds me,
the sound of horns,
quickly changing traffic lights,
speed, oh, so much terrible speed,
all alien to me, and so, so frightening.

I remember, Lord, when the highways and byways were quiet.
Like you, I went from town to town on foot.
Later, I rode a bicycle.

I chatted to your people along the way,
picked blackberries,
rested beneath the stars.

Now the traffic reports speak of congestion,
five-mile tailbacks and never-ending roadworks;
all is so alien to me,
I feel frightened.

Bless me, Lord, with companions on my journey:
gentle people who will help to keep me safe;
disciples of your kingdom who will draw me ever deeper into you.

Slow me down, Lord, to listen to your voice deep within my heart.
May I, whose life's path has been changed by dementia,
be a bearer of good news to all who cross my path
on my journey through life –
a journey we travel, hand in hand with you,
Lord and Master of my journey, Amen.

Carer’s prayers

A beautiful wife

My beautiful wife has dementia.
She was neither a good cook nor a very good housekeeper,
but she is a beautiful person,
beautiful within.
She has a beautiful spirit.
She has been my beautiful wife for 64 years,
I love her with every fibre of my being.
She is my beautiful wife.

A capable wife who can find?
She is far more precious than jewels.
The heart of her husband trusts in her.
(Proverbs 31:10, 11)

A carer's prayer

Love is patient; love is kind; love is not envious or boastful or arrogant or rude. It does not insist on its own way; it is not irritable or resentful; it does not rejoice in wrongdoing, but rejoices in the truth. It bears all things, believes all things, hopes all things, endures all things. Love never ends.

(1 Corinthians 13:4–8)

I felt so angry today, Lord.
The disability of my loved one wore me down and I nearly hit her.
I felt the level of my frustration rising;
I felt controlled and manipulated;
the confusion in my heart was tearing me apart.
I felt overwhelmed by the mixed messages of this awful journey;
do people understand what they do,
what they say,
or are they the victims of this awful disability?

Today, Lord, I felt a victim.
I know, Lord, the deep, heart-wrenching pain
I so often feel in the presence of Kate
and today, Lord, I wanted to lash out.
I was tired and almost lost control.
Once again I felt that my best efforts were not enough.
I felt alone and frightened by the intensity of my rage
and I almost gave way to my anger.
For so long now, every emotion and feeling
has felt crucified by what I see before me;
the cup of my patience is ebbing away.
The words 'it is always on your terms' had left my lips
before I had censored what I said;
But for once I thanked God for Kate's deafness.
She had not heard my cutting remark.
Stripped naked by my shame, I felt my vulnerability
as I had failed to respond with love.

The loss of control I was feeling was a tiny mirror image
of the loss that she and many with dementia suffer
so many times each day:
uncertainty, powerlessness, fear, despair, anguish.
Then I heard your words,
'Be angry, but do not sin.' [22]

I drew a breath and quietly walked away.

Please touch us, Lord,
and heal the pain of our breaking hearts.
Dry the tears that are too deep to share with anyone but you.
Pour your anointing oil over our spirits
so that through you we may be made whole.

Deepen my trust to depend on you to cope.
Like your apostle Paul
may I feel the power of Christ over me,
that I may respond in love and be an agent of healing
to all you have called me to serve.

I make this prayer in your name, O my Lord. Amen.

I pray that, according to the riches of his glory, he may grant that you may be strengthened in your inner being with power through his Spirit, and that Christ may dwell in your hearts through faith, as you are being rooted and grounded in love. I pray that you may have the power to comprehend, with all the saints, what is the breadth and length and height and depth, and to know the love of Christ that surpasses knowledge, so that you may be filled with all the fullness of God.

(Ephesians 3:16–19)

22. Ephesians 4:26

Gentleness

The Lord has comforted his people,
and will have compassion on his suffering ones.
(Isaiah 49:13)

Gentleness is the key to good dementia care.
Gentleness touches the spirit of the person
more fully than any other virtue.
A gentle caress reassures that they are not on their own;
others share the journey with them.

Gentleness asks that we be still
before each other and before God.
We lay down all our defences
and we embrace the spirit
and soul of the other.

We lay aside all self-seeking, all self-glorification, and
respond in love to all that is being asked of us
as we journey together to Emmaus.

We ask ourselves if we recognise Christ
in the stranger's guise,
when we may not understand the words
and actions of our companions.

Gentleness is the key to the soul, a free gift of the spirit.
Ask and it will be given to you, given free in love.

Care of the elderly

Then he went down with them and came to Nazareth, and was obedient to them. His mother treasured all these things in her heart. And Jesus increased in wisdom and in years, and in divine and human favour.

(Luke 2:51, 52)

I pray for all who struggle with the care of a loved one with
dementia, young or old.
I place before you their pain, frustration, grief, exhaustion and fear.
I place into the offertory plate the tears that are shed
as a loved one becomes ever more frail
and pray that these tears may be
transformed into a blessing of peace.

A blessing is born when one knows that one has faithfully
cared each step of the way.
It is a blessing when they have not walked away when the road
was rough, the future uncertain and the pain unbearable.

Send a blessing for all who hour after hour have kept faith and
stayed to keep watch with the suffering Christ;
whose courage did not fail when all seemed lost,
but who loved to their dying breath those who had borne them life.
They will know God's peace to the end of their days.

A wise child makes a glad father.
(Proverbs 10:1)

The washing

Jesus, knowing that the Father had given all things into his hands, and that he had come from God and was going to God, got up from the table, took off his outer robe, and tied a towel around himself. Then he poured water into a basin and began to wash the disciples' feet and to wipe them with the towel that was tied around him.

(John 13:3–5)

Lord, it is our privilege to wash the feet of our brothers and sisters with dementia. You have placed the care of your people into our hands and we thank you.

You washed the feet of your disciples as a parting gift,
an act of service, shortly before you returned to your Father.

You ministered to your disciples in humility and love.
You invite us to do the same.

You took some life-giving, life-renewing and healing water and poured it into a basin. In love, you washed your friend's dusty feet.

Each day we take water to wash each other's feet,
but do we do it with humility and love?

Has an act of service become another task to be completed quickly with little engagement with the person entrusted to our care?

Do we drop on our knees before a child of God
and minister to the person's needs with sensitivity,
gentleness and the milk of human kindness?

Is the scorn that is poured upon those with dementia
wiped away with compassion and care?

Does our busyness blind us to the tears
mingled with the soap-filled water?

Have our hearts hardened with indifference, coldness and fear?

Has the life-pulse in the feet we hold been snuffed out
by our slavery to policies, procedures and target-setting?

Our failure to notice the holy may lead us to ignore
the life story of your people before us;
the many miles that they have trod on your earth;
relationships formed, dreams realised,
hopes dashed, hopes renewed.

Loving Father, we pray that our relationship
and service are entirely of love.
We thank you for the wonderful sense of touch,
the opportunity to care,
to pour healing water and life-giving balm
over the body and spirit of your child.
We thank you that in this spirit our service is prayer.
We thank you that we become one with you
and one with each other through this washing.

We too have become one with you in the healing,
liberating and life-giving gift of the Eucharist
where you wash all our sins away.
We become a new creation in you.

Then he took a loaf of bread, and when he had given thanks, he broke it and gave it to them, saying, 'This is my body, which is given for you. Do this in remembrance of me.' And he did the same with the cup after supper, saying, 'This cup that is poured out for you is the new covenant in my blood.'

(Luke 22:19, 20)

Martha's prayer

'Lord, do you not care that my sister has left me to do all the work by myself? Tell her then to help me.'

(Luke 10:40)

My name is Martha, Lord.
I am the sister of Mary and Lazarus.
You know us as your life-long friends.
We rejoice in your friendship
and in our deep relationship with you.
We feel so privileged to be in your heart
and to share companionship with you.

As you journey on your mission of love you visit us
and come home to us when you are in need of rest.

Our door is always open to you and
we are so glad to welcome you into our home.

However, Lord, today I am struggling
and need to share my distress with you.
I believe that you will help me.

My sister, Mary, told me that she feels called
to a new mission to those with dementia.

She has learnt that there are many in our society
with memory problems, confusion, and different behaviours
and she wishes to pray for them and their families.

You know, Lord, how she wishes to spend so much time in prayer,
time in your presence, studying the scriptures,
reflecting and being silent before God.
She amazes me because she could pray 24 hours a day
if I allowed her to do so!

However, you who worked as a carpenter in your Father's shed
know that time spent in contemplation alone
does not bring water from the well or place food on the table.
I feel isolated and alone in my homemaking duties.
I do not wish to get angry with her, because she has a good heart,
a heart so full of love, and now she wishes to support
those who suffer so much on the margins of our society.

You understand being on the margins, Lord.
You have been pushed there so often.
But dinner needs to be cooked today!

Once again, Lord, I am frustrated at being on my own
with pots and pans, and cry out to you to hear my prayer.
'Lord, do you not care that my sister is leaving me
to do the serving all by myself?
Please tell her to help me.'
As with so many carers, my patience is wearing thin.
I am tired, weary and lonely as I move through the daily grind.
I do not understand this new disability of which she speaks
and just wish that she would help me now!
The words 'lost', 'trapped' and 'victim' spring to mind,
and I wish that she could enter more fully into my reality.

Suddenly your gentle voice breaks through the mist
that has clouded my mind.
I hear you speak to me of your kingdom,
of a new form of listening and of being with you;
a listening in deep silence at your feet,
listening that leads to deep inner transformation,
frees me from all worry, anxiety and fear;
a listening that calls me to trust that all will be well
and that I do not need to be fretful about the mundane things of life.
'Martha, Martha,' you said, 'you worry and fret about so many
things and yet few are needed, indeed only one.'
You remind me that so many of these details are not important
and that my sister, Mary, has found the pearl of great price,
'and it is not to be taken from her'.

I thank you for your words of love and reassurance.
I thank you for what you are teaching me
through my sister's deep relationship with you.
I thank you for her new mission to those with dementia.
I place before you all carers
who struggle with the daily heartaches of their role
and ask you to bless each one.
Please remind them that they are not alone
and that you are with them each step of the way.
Be with them in their isolation, tiredness, loneliness
and fear of an unknown future.
Bless them, Lord, with a peace that can only be found
sitting at your feet and trusting in your infinite love,
a peace enclosed in a pearl beyond price;
a pearl that cannot be taken from them.
This, Lord, has been a gift from Mary to me,
which she has learnt from those with dementia,
and we thank you.
We thank you, you who are the pearl of greatest price.[23]

23. Scripture references in this reflection adapted from Luke 10:38–42

Guide dogs for the blind

They came to Bethsaida. Some people brought a blind man to him and begged him to touch him. He took the blind man by the hand and led him out of the village.

(Mark 8:22, 23)

Lord, today you guided my friend and I to the
guide dog training centre.
You invited us to come and see the wonderful work
that is done for people with blindness and reduced vision.
Blind people trust you to care for them through your creation.

Our visit was inspired by my friend's love of dogs.
He is living with Alzheimer's disease.
His first symptoms revealed themselves when he was 34 years old.
To me he is a witness of a man
who wishes to embrace life in all its fullness,
a man who despite major loss never gives way
to self-pity, negativity or bitterness,
a gentleman whose spirit is enriched by contact
with beautiful canine friends.

Care, compassion and total commitment to the
wellbeing of the blind radiated from every person
at the guide dog training centre.
The fascinating life-story of the guide dog was
shared with enthusiasm and joy.
Great attention is paid to the detail of the lives
of blind people and their four-legged friends.
Dogs are carefully bred and chosen for the people
whose lives they will share and whose eyes they will become.

The dogs go into strict training to achieve their goal
and to be the best servant and friend to their host.
The prize they wish to capture is the safety and joy of their master.

They carry a high price tag.
It costs £40,000 to support a blind person
with a dog for life.
Not one single penny is received from the Government
to support this essential work.

A guide dog is willing to lay down its life for its host
and does not count the cost.

The gentle relationship of my friend
and the dogs was beautiful to see.
There was an immediate connection between man and beast.
Communication was real, natural, spontaneous.

Joy was shared and spirits were renewed.

Beautiful, strong animals did not confront my friend
with his disability.
Acceptance was mutual and total.
No questions asked,
no judgements made,
no fears triggered,
no demons released.

The Lord of all creation walked on the earth.
He came to offer new sight to the blind
and touched some of the blindness of my own spirit.
I prayed that scales would fall from my own eyes
and that I would be set free.
I asked for the gift to look with gratitude at what lay before me.

I know that all too often I am not able to
lay down my life for my friends;
all too often the cost of being a servant touches
the wounds of my resistance;
I am led astray by my own sin.

I may bark in frustration and not rest at my Master's feet.
A price of £40,000 of service is beyond my reach.

As light fades and all before me becomes dull,
you reach out your healing hand,
you put spittle on my eyes and you lay your hands on me,[24]
you bless me in your embrace;
I hear again, or even for the first time, your healing words:

'Receive your sight.'

Your good news of salvation touches my soul.

I recognise that this visit might never have taken place
if I had not been led to the centre by my friend.

I know that I have been blessed by my friend and I am grateful.

24. Mark 8:23

My daughter

My beautiful daughter has a prion,
a rare genetic disease.
This has ravaged her entire body with dementia
and robbed her of so much dignity.
This cruel disease stole my wife at 44,
robbed my little girl of her mother.
A visitation has now fallen on my little child,
she who is only 36 years old.
I am 73 years old.
My heart breaks within me.

My anguish is unbearable
at the suffering she carries.
Memory fails her,
balance is poor;
screams and shouts ring out throughout the day,
far into the night.
She cries,
my heart breaks within me.

So often she fails to know me as her father.
Beautiful sons are robbed of their mother,
her partner is at a loss how to live
without the woman he loves.
My heart breaks within me.

Is she asleep or has she died to my love?
I pray the words of you, my Lord:
'Little girl, get up!'[25]
break forth from your chains,
come back to me,
know my love.

25 Mark 5:41

You come to me, my Lord,
lay your hands on my heart,
speak words of calm,
fill me with a presence I have never known before.
You who are Love have taken my little one in your arms,
blessed her,
bestowed your healing promise upon her;
a healing not of this world,
a healing of your kingdom deep within her soul,
healing that has bound up all broken hearts,
in a deep knowledge of your mysterious love,
you who are love.

'Let the little children come to me; do not stop them; for it is to such as these that the kingdom of God belongs.'

(Mark 10:14)

Thou shalt not steal

Give your strength to your servant;
save the child of your serving-maid.
Show me a sign of your favour,
so that those who hate me may see it and be put to shame,
because you, Lord, have helped me and comforted me.
(Psalm 86:16, 17)

I cry out to you, my Lord.
In your kindness bend your ear and hear my prayer.
My spirit is anguished because our home was raided today.

My darling wife has quickly advancing Alzheimer's disease.
We live together on the outskirts of a city.
We have both passed the biblical age of 70
and have reached the age of 80,
your kind allocation of life to those who are strong.
Our four adult children have left home and we are alone.

We had gone to town on the bus
to celebrate the Eucharist with you.

Our joy at receiving you in the Eucharist is great,
a joy that we savour every moment of our day.
In you we live and move and have our being.

You feed us with your word,
enrich us in our poverty and
bless us with your peace.

We returned home to find that somebody
had forced open a window,
ransacked our home and violated our privacy.
Intruders who had forgotten
'You shall not steal.' [26]

26. Exodus 20:15

Our treasured possessions were strewn around the house,
cupboards ransacked;
evil had tarnished our sacred space.
Some items had been taken,
but the greater wound is the sense that
our personal and domestic safety has been threatened.

We are fragile and vulnerable.
We have no answer to those who have placed our lives in danger.

We cry out to you, Lord, for healing and peace.
Peace for our wounded hearts,
peace for our wounded minds,
minds that have been savagely attacked by this act of violence;
peace for a broken world,
a world that sees no evil in the assault
of the elderly and most vulnerable.
We cry out to you, Lord, and ask that
you forgive them, for 'they do not know what they are doing'.[27]

May they know a conversion of heart and be healed.

May I who have been asked by you
to walk an Alzheimer's journey with my beloved,
be an agent of peace and reconciliation for
the perpetrator of this horrible crime.
May the suffering we bear because of her disability
be an act of reparation
for all who have walked far from your law.
May the tears we weep mingle with your blood of atonement.
May we, your people, be washed clean
in the redeeming blood of the Lamb.

May we all be one.

27. Luke 23:34

The Tree of Peace

This is what I saw;
there was a tree at the centre of the earth, and its height was great.
The tree grew great and strong, its top reached to heaven,
and it was visible to the ends of the whole earth.
Its foliage was beautiful, its fruit abundant,
and it provided food for all.
The animals of the field found shade under it,
the birds of the air nested in its branches,
and from it all living beings were fed.
(Daniel 4:10–12)

My friend has dementia;
life is often a struggle for her.
This morning she was very distressed.
She had mislaid her purse and feared that it had been stolen.
She asked me to help her.
I was at a loss to comfort her.

I prayed for a moment and asked
your Holy Spirit to guide us.

I looked out of the window and noticed
that it was a beautiful spring day.
Nature invited us outside.

I invited my friend to take a walk with me.

After a moment's hesitation she agreed.

We stepped into another world;
a world free from anxiety,
a different space.

The air was crisp;
daffodils were beginning to burst forth through the soil;
abundant gifts lay waiting for us.

It was good to be alive.
We walked slowly.
Her life story unfolded.
She had many happy childhood memories,
memories which she wished to share.
Adult life too had been blessed.
She was grateful
and invited me ever more deeply
into her own happy world.

It was good to be with her,
to learn from her,
to walk beside her,
to listen and learn a little more of who she is,
to learn a little more of who I am.

The lost purse was never mentioned.
She was at peace.

A profound moment of grace awaited us.
We came upon a tree with little buds on its branches.
She noticed it first.
She reached out to the little buds with great gentleness.
She smiled;
she praised you, O God,
for the beauty between her fingertips;
peace exuded from her soul.

I watched in silence,
reflected on your saving presence with us.

I remembered another saving tree,
the Tree of Life.
They took you out and hung you on a tree.
You cried out in a loud voice and said,
'Father, into your hands I commend my spirit.'[28]

Three days later you rose from the dead,
you offered us life for ever.

28. Luke 23:46

I believe, Lord, that my friend has united
her prayer of surrender with yours.
Her spirit is totally given over to you.

She sees your beauty in so many things;
she gives you thanks.
Our lives are blessed through her;
we give you thanks.

We returned home.
Her purse was lying on her bed.
She was at peace;
agitation had evaporated before the tree,
distress was no more.

We praise you for your tree,
a tree of abundant life,
a tree of hope,
a tree of healing,
the Tree of Peace.

Goodnight, my love

Goodnight, my love, goodnight,
goodnight, my love, goodnight
goodnight, my love.

'Master, now you are dismissing your servant in peace,
according to your word;
for my eyes have seen your salvation,
which you have prepared in the presence of all peoples,
a light for revelation to the Gentiles
and for glory to your people Israel.'
(Luke 2:29–32)

Prayers of general intercession

Tears

'Are you in tears yet?'
These words were spoken by the world-famous author Terry Pratchett
as he stumbled through a public reading of one of his books.

Millions of TV viewers were deeply touched
by his humility as he shared his struggle
with what he called 'this horrible illness, Alzheimer's disease'.
He pleaded with all not to rob him of his identity
and call him 'Mr Alzheimer's'.

Lord, we beg your forgiveness for the many times
we rob one another of true identity
by labelling each other with negative, abusive labels.

So often we diminish your life in others by focusing
on the weakness, brokenness and vulnerability of another.

For a moment we forget or decide not to see your face
in our brother or sister.
We do not acknowledge that
each is made in your image and likeness
and shares in your glory.

You have placed your cross on their shoulders
and in our blindness we fail to see
your struggle in their struggle.

We pray for a spirit of repentance to weep with those who weep.

May we support each person's struggle;
may we know a conversion of heart
and by the wounds of others may we be healed.

Let us understand with our hearts, be converted and be healed.[29]

29. See Isaiah 6:10

Our Father

'Lord, teach us to pray just as John taught his disciples.' *(Luke 11:1)*

Dear Father in heaven,
we give thanks for the many lovely memories we hold of our fathers.
The gift that they are/were to us was bestowed on us by you.

Hallowed be your name.
May we mention your name and their names
with respect and deep love.

Your kingdom come,
may the reign of God enfold our world.

Your will be done on earth;
may your will of supporting all with a dementia disability
be done on earth,

As it is in heaven.
May all who suffer be honoured with heavenly respect.

Give us this day our daily bread;
we ask for the bread of wisdom, insight, gentleness and
compassion that we need to support all affected by dementia.

And forgive us our trespasses,
of indifference, neglect, complacency and fear
in our relationships with your broken people.
Grace us, Lord,
with a spirit of forgiveness for those who dismiss and deride
our support of the vulnerable.

Lead us not into the temptation
to give up on our support of those entrusted to our care.

Deliver us from
a fear of the future, knowing that
you are with us until the end of time.
Amen.

Friendship

After leaving the synagogue he entered Simon's house. Now Simon's mother-in-law was suffering from a high fever, and they asked him about her. Then he stood over her and rebuked the fever, and it left her. Immediately she got up and began to serve them.

(Luke 4:38, 39)

Lord, we thank you for all who faithfully visit
those affected by dementia.
We pray in gratitude for the loyalty of friendship,
for moments of joy shared,
for smiles, hugs and laughter, knowing that

the light of the eyes rejoices the heart
and good news refreshes the body.

(Proverbs 15:30)

For quiet presence,
for the gift of prayer,
for carer respite,
for words of encouragement and practical tasks undertaken,
for day trips and lifetime photo albums shared,
we give you thanks for the gift of love
which is the elixir of life.
May we be a friend to those who need a friend,
modelling our friendship on your friendship to all.

'The Spirit of the Lord is upon me,
because he has anointed me
to bring good news to the poor.
He has sent me to proclaim release to the captives
and recovery of sight to the blind,
to let the oppressed go free,
to proclaim the year of the Lord's favour.'

(Luke 4:18, 19)

Holiness

Supplications, prayers, intercessions, and thanksgivings should be made for everyone, for kings and all who are in high positions, so that we may lead a quiet and peaceable life in all godliness and dignity. This is right and is acceptable in the sight of God our Saviour.

(1 Timothy 2:1–4)

Today, Lord, we pray for all who write Government policies
and procedures for those with dementia.

We pray that they hear the cry of all who reach out to them
for understanding and practical support.

We pray that they may hear the distress of those
who because of disability are no longer able to work,
who struggle to pay their bills and whose lives
have been robbed of a certain dignity.
You, Lord, worked with your hands and understand
the dignity and value of human labour.

Loneliness and boredom may have crept into their day
and they may feel distant from themselves and others:
'I am so bored – I was able to travel the world with my job
and now I sit in my flat unable to work.'

These good people may question an uncertain future
and not know where to turn for help.

We pray, Lord, that you bestow on your holy ones
people of great wisdom and insight who will
act justly,
love tenderly
and walk humbly with you[30]
in their service of your saints.

30. See Micah 6:8

We pray that they may hear the words 'I thirst' and respond
with efficiency, effectiveness, courtesy and care.

We pray that real or imagined financial constraints
will not impede a service of love
and that your little ones will be helped in real and practical ways
to walk free from anything that is not of you.

We pray that our policy-makers, health-care professionals and all
your servants may incarnate the prayer of Paul:

'May he so strengthen your hearts in holiness that you may be
blameless before our God and Father at the coming of our
Lord Jesus with all his saints.'

(1 Thessolonians 3:13)

Amen.

Resources

Alzheimer's disease

Introduction

The purpose of this section is to give a brief overview of facts about Alzheimer's disease and provide an insight into a carer's perspective.

What is Alzheimer's disease?

Alzheimer's disease is a progressive, degenerative disease and the most common form of dementia. It is caused by irreversible brain damage and proceeds in stages over months or years, gradually destroying memory, reason, judgement and language. The ability to carry out simple tasks is also eventually destroyed.

Interesting facts

- It is named after Dr Alois Alzheimer, a German doctor who presented the first case of the disease in 1906.
- It can affect people as young as 30, but this is very rare.
- Up to the age of 65 it affects 1 in 1000 people.
- Over the age of 65 it affects 5 in 500 people.
- Over the age of 80 it affects 20 in 100 people.

Diagnosis

There is no simple test to make a diagnosis. However, by taking a careful history of a person's problem from a close relative or friend, together with an examination of the person's physical and mental state, a provisional diagnosis can be made.

It is important to exclude other treatable conditions that may cause memory loss. These may include:

- depression
- urinary or chest infections
- vitamin deficiency
- brain tumour.

Treatment

No treatment at present can stop Alzheimer's disease. However, for some people in the early and mid stages of the disease, the drug Aricept may slow the progression of the disease for a limited time. Response to medication varies from person to person.

Some medications may help with behavioural symptoms such as agitation, sleeplessness, excessive walking, depression and aggression.

The three stages of Alzheimer's

Early stage symptoms

At this stage the dementia may be overlooked and incorrectly diagnosed as 'old age'.

- Short-term memory loss
- Difficulty performing familiar tasks
- Problems with speech
- Disorientation in time and place
- Poor or decreased judgement
- Problems keeping track of things
- Misplacing things
- Changes in mood or behaviour
- Changes in personality
- Loss of initiative

Middle stage symptoms

The problems become more evident, the person having increasing difficulty coping with day-to-day living.

- Can no longer manage to live alone
- Is unable to cook, clean or shop
- May become extremely dependent
- Needs assistance with personal hygiene, i.e., washing, bathing, and toileting
- Needs help with dressing
- Increasing difficulty with speech
- Walks a lot and may get lost
- Shows behaviour abnormalities such as unprovoked aggression.
- May experience hallucinations

Late stage symptoms

The person becomes totally dependent and inactive. Memory problems are very serious and the person becomes increasingly disabled.

- Difficulty eating
- Does not recognise relatives, friends or familiar objects
- Has difficulty understanding or interpreting events
- May be unable to find his/her way around the home
- Walks a great deal and may get lost
- Has difficulty walking
- Suffers bladder and bowel incontinence
- Inappropriate behaviour in public
- Is confined to a wheelchair or bed
- Becomes totally dependent

How do we care appropriately?

Caring for a person with Alzheimer's disease can be very difficult and extremely stressful at times. However, there are ways to deal with the situation. The following information may be useful; it stems from discussion with other carers, both family and professional.

Maintain dignity

In the early stages the person may be aware of struggling with everyday tasks that once seemed easy. What you and others say can have a profound effect on the dignity of the person.

Establish routines

Keeping a routine can help prompt the person into remembering what he or she meant to be doing, bringing order and structure into a challenging situation.

Support independence

The person with dementia should be encouraged to remain independent for as long as possible, for example, by going shopping, carrying out household tasks, making decisions. (Some support may be needed with some of these tasks, but people benefit from being given the opportunity to do as much as they can.)

Simplify tasks

Try to make things simple. Do not offer too many choices, as this may confuse and upset the person with dementia. Try to simplify daily routines.

Improve safety

As the disease progresses, loss of physical co-ordination and memory increase the chance of injury. Common hazards include loose carpets, polished floors, trailing electrical cables and clutter. Gas cookers and coal fires can also present a hazard and are best avoided if possible. Reducing the risk of accidents is important.

Keep active

Some planned activities can enhance a person's sense of dignity and self worth by giving purpose and meaning to life. A person may gain satisfaction from using skills related to a previous occupation or hobby.

Communication

People whose language becomes impaired rely more on other senses such as sight and touch. Make sure that the person's senses such as eyesight and hearing are not impeded. Speak clearly, slowly, face to face and at eye level. Show love and warmth through facial expression or appropriate touch. Pay attention to the person's body language; people whose language is impaired communicate through non-verbal means. Be aware of your own body language. Make sure that you have the person's attention before speaking.

Avoid confrontation

Any type of conflict causes unnecessary stress on you and the person with Alzheimer's disease. People with this disease will invariably forget or deny that they have done something 'wrong'. It is important to remember that this problem is caused by the illness. Avoid drawing attention to failure and maintain a calm composure. Avoid confrontation. The person may forget the incident, but the painful feelings associated with confrontation may persist long after you have forgotten the dispute. This may cause great distress that the person is not able to verbalise.

Memory aids

One of the main problems with Alzheimer's disease is the failure of short-term memory. A useful way of helping the person is to create personalised 'memory joggers' such as:

- photographs of family or close friends
- boards showing day, date, time of next meal
- large clock showing the correct time
- familiar objects kept in their usual place, easily found
- message board in a prominent place
- list of simple instructions for everyday routines.

Facts from the Alzheimer's Society

Keeping active and staying involved

As a person's dementia develops it is likely to have an impact on some abilities, but there will still be lots that the person can enjoy doing, both individually and with others. Maintaining existing skills, as far as possible, can give the person pleasure and boost confidence. For this reason it is important to help find activities that the person enjoys doing, and to continually adapt them to meet the person's changing interests and needs throughout the illness.

The word 'activities' is often associated with structured group activities such as bingo or exercise classes, but not everyone enjoys this type of pursuit. In fact, many beneficial activities are the simple, everyday tasks that many of us take for granted, which may be enjoyed as a solitary pastime or in pairs or small groups. Simple activities such as taking a walk, polishing a pair of shoes, listening to the radio or looking after a pet can help give pleasure and bring purpose to the day.

What is good for people with dementia is often good for those who spend time with them too. Through helping maintain the interests of the person with dementia, family members and carers may be able to follow their own interests. Keeping occupied and stimulated can improve quality of life for people with dementia as well as those around them.

Benefits to the person with dementia

- Remaining physically and mentally active can have a significant impact on a person's wellbeing. It can provide a welcome distraction from the stresses of the illness and can help the person focus on the positive and fun aspects of life.
- Carrying out routine tasks can help people with dementia feel better about themselves by providing a structure to the day and a sense of achievement.

- Some types of activity can help the person to express feelings – for example listening to music, doing a sketch or writing something down.

Benefits to loved ones and carers

- Boredom and frustration are the two most common causes of challenging behaviour in people with dementia. If a person with dementia is occupied and stimulated some of the behaviour that those around the person find most difficult may lessen or even stop altogether.
- Sharing an activity that both parties enjoy may bring them closer together and help them find new ways to relate to each other.
- Discovering new ways to stimulate someone with dementia can be satisfying, and may enable those around the person to think differently about their caring role.

Finding suitable activities

If you want to help people with dementia to take part in some activities, talk to them about which activities they might still enjoy that they could achieve within their current capabilities. Try to find imaginative ways to adapt their activities to their changing capabilities and moods. Popular ideas include:

Exercise

Exercising together will be beneficial to the person with dementia and anyone accompanying him or her. Exercise burns up the adrenalin produced by stress and frustration, and produces endorphins that can promote feelings of happiness. This will help both parties relax and increase their sense of wellbeing. Exercise helps develop a healthy appetite, increases energy levels and promotes a better night's sleep.

- Walking is a great form of exercise that provides a change of scene and fresh air. Short walks can make a big difference, even if only to post a letter or go to a local coffee shop.
- Swimming is another good all-round exercise, and the feeling of being in the water can be very soothing and calming.

- Classes may be suitable if the person wants something more sociable. Find out if your local leisure or community centre offers suitable classes for older people with dementia.

Reminders of the past

People with dementia can often remember the distant past more easily than recent events. If you can find a way to help trigger the more distant, pleasant memories, the person may become more animated and interested. Not everyone enjoys reminiscing about the past, but the following suggestions might be useful for those who do.

- Talk about the past together, while looking at old family photos or books with pictures or listening to music.
- Make up a memory or rummage box of objects that the person with dementia might be interested in. Physically handling things may trigger memories more effectively than looking at pictures.
- A visit to a favourite place might also prompt happy memories and provide another opportunity to get out and about.
- Be aware that talking about the past in this way can sometimes trigger strong emotions in the person you care for, so it's important to be sensitive. You may uncover painful memories as well as happy ones.
- Dementia damages the memory and the thinking and reasoning parts of the brain, but the emotions remain intact. It is not necessarily a bad thing if the person becomes emotional, but if so make sure you allow these feelings to be expressed, and acknowledge them.
- Avoid asking very specific questions that require factual responses and could put the person on the spot – the main aim is to enjoy the memories rather than to make the person feel tested in any way.

Activities during the early stages of dementia

Someone in the early stages of dementia may want to continue doing the things he or she has always done. People with dementia retain memory for some activities, depending upon which part of the brain has been damaged. Activities such as reading, typing or playing the piano are not always affected.

If you are close to someone with early dementia, be aware of the danger of taking over jobs and tasks too quickly in an attempt to minimise your own stress. For example, if the person does the washing up, accept that it might not get done to the standard that you would normally like; recognise that the person will feel good about making a useful contribution – and that is what is important.

Other tips include:

- Encourage the person to enjoy activities unaided.
- Provide encouragement and reminders.
- Put any equipment in a place where the person can see it and reach it easily.
- When you suggest what to do, use short sentences.
- Set aside time in the day when you are going to focus on doing something enjoyable for both of you away from the normal routines of the day.

Involving others

Consider inviting other people (including paid workers, family members or volunteers) to spend time with the person to do something they both enjoy – for example, going for a walk or playing a game of cards. If you are the sole carer, you might find it hard to hand over and trust others, but they may bring a fresh approach that the person may resonate with in new ways. When you are a full-time carer it can be hard to have the energy to always give 'quality time' to the person if you are exhausted and stressed.

Activity ideas

- *Craft activities* – These might include activities such as creating collages from magazines, or knitting. Someone who has been a skilful knitter may still be able to knit squares for a blanket.
- *Puzzles* – Someone who has enjoyed doing crosswords may still enjoy a puzzle book.
- *Doing things together* – The person may like to play cards or board games, or you could do some gardening or baking together.

- *Activities around the home* – Men and women alike can enjoy helping with washing and drying up, setting the table or making beds. Again, the result may not be perfect, but it can give an important sense of achievement. The person might be surprisingly interested in odd jobs such as sorting through a drawer or a toolbox.
- *Music* – Even when other abilities are severely affected, many people still enjoy singing, dancing and listening to music. Record a collection of the person's favourite pieces of music or songs to listen to.
- *TV and radio* – Many people with dementia enjoy listening to the radio. Television, however, can cause problems. Some people with dementia lose the ability to tell the difference between what is real and what is on screen, and can become distressed. They can also become confused by too much noise. Try watching television together, and choose programmes with small sections of action or humour, rather than a programme with an involved plot. Some people have found using headphones can help them to concentrate better. However, for some people even a favourite soap opera may become confusing.
- *Communal activities* – If the person has a connection with an organisation within the local community, whether it is a church, a pub or a club, then continuing to visit this place might be very important. It may help if a family member or carer has some gentle discussions with other attendees to encourage them to continue to welcome the person with dementia, and to minimise any embarrassment.

Some people with dementia come into their own in certain social situations in a way that can surprise those close to them. However, others become daunted by being away from the safety of their own home and avoid going out. If the person seems reluctant to join in, don't always take the first 'no' for an answer, as people will sometimes just say 'no' as the safest option and will actually enjoy themselves if pushed a little to take the step out of the door. However, don't force them to do something that they clearly don't enjoy.

Activities during the later stages of dementia

As people's dementia advances they will still be able to carry out some tasks that are very familiar to them, but will probably be more interested in the process of doing the activity than in the result. If this is the case with someone close to you, look for 'magic moments' throughout the day rather than trying to carry out sustained activities. Keeping your expectations realistic and enjoying these moments may help you at a difficult time of adjusting to the many changes in the person.

Activity ideas

- Look for activities that are stimulating but that don't involve too many challenges or choices. People with dementia can find it difficult to process options.
- Many people with dementia retain their sense of humour, so look for activities that the person with dementia, and those caring for them, will find entertaining. Having a good laugh will do everyone good. This might mean discovering your own playful or silly side, which some people find easier than others.
- Dementia often affects people's concentration so that they can't focus on what they are doing for very long; it may be a good idea to do activities in short bursts.
- Dementia can affect people's motivation. You may have to help them get started, but try not to be disheartened.
- Break instructions into small, manageable chunks, and make sure each step of the task is very simple.
- Try to think of activities that involve an easy, repetitive action and simple steps, such as sweeping, dusting or winding wool.

Sensory stimulation

During the later stages of their dementia, people often develop severe difficulties with reasoning and language, but they will still have their sense of taste, touch and smell. There are various things you can do to stimulate these senses – for example:

- Encourage the person to touch or stroke pieces of fabric, dolls or cuddly toys.

- Try giving the person a hand massage, using a scented oil such as lavender. This can be very soothing for those who enjoy touch.
- Continue to take the time to sit and talk to the person or to read out loud. Much anecdotal evidence suggests that a person remains able to hear you talking very late into the progression of the illness.
- Enable the person to see a fish tank, mobile or a window with a nice view. This may have a calming effect.
- Make sure the person has a regular change of scene and the stimulation of the fresh air and the outdoor environment. If you are visiting a person living in a care home, you can still play a vital role in helping that person to feel included and active, even if it is only to take a short walk with them down the corridor or to bring in something of interest from outside the home.

Your local Alzheimer's Society branch will always be willing to talk to you and offer advice and information to support your needs.

Dementia Catalogue, a specialist dementia information resource, is available at alzheimers.org.uk/dementiacatalogue

Driving and dementia

People who have been diagnosed with dementia may be able to continue driving for some time. However, they must fulfil certain legal requirements. When their condition deteriorates to the point that they are unsafe on the road they must stop driving. Many people find this very difficult to accept. This section explains the legal situation, and gives some tips on stopping driving.

Can a person with dementia still drive?

A diagnosis of dementia is not in itself necessarily a reason to stop driving. What matters, from both a legal and a practical point of view, is whether or not an individual is still able to drive safely.

For experienced drivers, driving may seem to be a largely automatic activity. In fact, driving is a complicated task that requires a split-second combination of complex thought processes and manual skills. To drive, a person needs to be able to:

- make sense of and respond to everything seen
- 'read the road'
- follow road signs
- anticipate and react quickly to the actions of other road users
- take appropriate action to avoid accidents
- remember where one is going.

Many people with dementia retain learned skills and are able to drive safely for some time after diagnosis. However, as dementia progresses it has serious effects on memory, perception and the ability to perform even simple tasks. People with dementia will, therefore, eventually lose the ability to drive. The stage at which this happens will be different for each person.

What if people are unsure of their ability to drive?

People with a diagnosis of dementia who are unsure of their ability to continue driving can take a driving assessment. To do this, they need to apply directly to an assessment centre, and pay a fee. For details of assessment centres, see 'Useful organisations', page 109.

An assessment is not like a driving test. It is an overall assessment of the impact that the dementia is having on a person's driving performance and safety, and it makes some allowances for the bad habits that drivers get into.

Giving up driving

Many people with dementia choose to stop driving because they begin to find it stressful or they lose confidence. A person should consider stopping driving if feeling:

- less confident or more irritated when driving
- confused if there are road works, for example, on a familiar route
- worried about having an accident.

People who feel like this will need support and understanding from their carer and family members. They may feel bad about stopping driving if they are accustomed to being independent, or if they have always driven their partners or family around. However, it is better to travel safely on public transport than risk an accident in a car. A person with dementia who decides to stop driving should return the licence to the Driver and Vehicle Licensing Agency (DVLA) – see 'Useful organisations', page 109.

Continuing to drive

Someone who receives a diagnosis of dementia and wants to continue to drive must, by law, inform the DVLA. Notification of the diagnosis should be sent with the person's full name, address, date of birth and the driver number on the driving licence, if known, to the Drivers Medical Group – see 'Useful organisations', page 109.

The DVLA will send the person a questionnaire that seeks permission for the DVLA to obtain medical reports from the person's GP and/or consultant. Once the person returns this questionnaire, the DVLA will contact his or her consultant (or, if no consultant details are provided, the GP). Based on the medical information it receives, it will make a decision as to whether the person can continue to drive. The DVLA may also ask the person to take a driving assessment.

A person with a diagnosis of dementia would be breaking the law by not telling the DVLA about the diagnosis, and could be fined up to £1000. If a person with dementia does not inform the DVLA about the diagnosis and continues to drive against advice from a doctor, the doctor may inform the DVLA if he or she feels that public safety or road safety would be at risk. Other people such as family members, neighbours or police officers may also contact the DVLA in writing and ask it to carry out a medical investigation if they are concerned about a person's fitness to drive.

People with a diagnosis of dementia must also immediately inform their car insurance company. If they do not, their policies may become invalid. It is a criminal offence to drive without at least third party cover.

When the DVLA decides that the person can continue driving

If, following its medical enquiry, the DVLA decides that the person can continue to drive, they will issue a new driving licence that will be valid for a limited period. For someone with dementia, the licence duration is usually for one year, although in very early cases it may be longer, up to a maximum of three years. The person's condition will be reviewed at least once a year. It is also a good idea for relatives, or others close to the person with dementia, to tactfully monitor the person's driving skills on a regular basis.

Reducing the risks

Someone with dementia can take steps to minimise the risk through driving. Short drives on familiar roads at quiet times of day generally present fewer problems than long, unfamiliar journeys or journeys in heavy traffic.

Key for disabled toilets

Across the country there are 1000 disabled toilets provided by local authorities. They are often kept locked to prevent misuse and vandalism, but keys can be purchased, allowing independent access.

They are useful when the carer taking a person with a dementia out is a different sex and therefore cannot go into the toilet. Obtainable from RADAR, 12 City Forum, 250 City Road, London EC1V 8AF: 020 7250 3222 or radar@radar.org.uk

Wheelchairs

If you consider a wheelchair necessary, consult your GP.

Incontinence pads

Contact your local district nursing service, through your GP, for assessment of requirements.

Free eye tests in your own home

These are for all those who cannot visit an optician unattended, including people with dementia. Telephone: 0500 295 245

Blue Badge Scheme

If the person you care for has serious mobility problems or is unsafe to walk independently because of confusion, it may be posible to get a special permit for easier public parking. Telephone your local council for more details.

Financial issues

People living with dementia and their carers may have specific financial needs. Help is available through the following benefits (information from Dementia UK).

Attendance allowance

A benefit paid to people who need help with personal care – including personal hygiene, getting dressed and medication – or who need support or supervision. It is not means tested and is paid to the person with dementia. It is paid at two rates; the higher rate is paid if the person needs help during the night. Attendance allowance forms are available by phoning 0845 712 3456 or Freephone 0800 882 200; successful claims are backdated to the date of the call. It is easier to get through on the phone in the late afternoon.
http://www.direct.gov.uk/en/DisabledPeople/FinancialSupport/DG_10012442

Disability living allowance

A benefit paid to people who need help either with personal care or with mobility or both. It is not means tested and is applicable to people under the age of 65. A person with dementia who reaches the age of 65 will still receive this and does not change over to attendance allowance. There may also be a mobility component in the payment if necessary. Forms are available by phoning 0845 712 3456 or Freephone 0800 882 200.
http://www.direct.gov.uk/en/DisabledPeople/FinancialSupport/DisabilityLivingAllowance/index.htm

Employment and support allowance

Check with your Job Centre for the most up-to-date information.

Council tax reduction

If people with dementia receive either attendance allowance or disability living allowance at middle or higher rate, they are exempt from paying council tax. Phone the council tax department and ask for further details on reductions. This is not means tested.

Severe Disability Premium

Details available from the Department of Work and Pensions or the benefits helpline: 0845 712 3456.
http://www.direct.gov.uk/en/DisabledPeople/FinancialSupport/OtherBenefitsAndSupport/DG_068683

Carer's Allowance

A benefit paid to the carer of someone in receipt of attendance allowance or disability living allowance. The carer must spend 35 hours per week caring for someone, and have earned less than £100 per week, once allowable expenses are deducted. Further details on entitlement and how to apply are available from 0845 608 4321.
http://www.direct.gov.uk/en/CaringForSomeone/MoneyMatters/CarersAllowance/index.htm

Carer's credit

Available if you offer care for 20 hours but not 35 hours a week. For details phone 0845 608 4321.
http://www.direct.gov.uk/en/CaringForSomeone/MoneyMatters/DG_10037637

Benefits calculator

This is an online calculator, which can be used to see the benefits you or someone else might be entitled to receive: www.direct.gov.uk – click on Benefits Adviser.

Appointeeship

It may be possible to arrange a person's pension or benefits to be paid to the carer when there is good reason. Contact the Department of Work and Pensions (DWP – formerly DSS): 0845 606 0265.

Direct payments/personal budget scheme

Please check about details of eligibility for direct payments with your local Social Services Department.

Ten Christmas survival tips for families coping with dementia

For most families, Christmas is a time for family gatherings, sharing laughter and happy memories. But for family caregivers of those living with dementia, Christmas can bring stress, disappointment, sadness and frustration.

Because of the changes a person with dementia has experienced, he or she may feel a sense of loss during Christmas. At the same time caregivers may feel obliged to maintain traditions and feel overwhelmed in the process. Families may feel uncertain when they start to recognise the changes in their loved one during their visit.

1. Planning can avoid Christmas stress

As Christmas approaches, give thought to the challenges that might be encountered. Consider ahead what may be expected of you, both socially and emotionally.

- Discuss celebrations with relatives and close friends in advance.
- Plan to maintain a regular routine while trying to provide a pleasant, meaningful and calm Christmas.
- Celebrate early in the day or have a noon meal rather than a late dinner.

2. Take care of yourself (caregiver)

Remember, Christmas is an opportunity to share time with people you love. Try to make the celebrations easy on yourself and the person with dementia so that you may concentrate on enjoying your time together.

- Set limits by telling family and friends that you intend to control stress this Christmas.
- Maintain a positive mental attitude.
- Ask for assistance for you and your loved one.

- Contact local services for advice and support.
- Prepare to deal with post-Christmas let-down. Arrange for family or friend support so you can enjoy a break (even for a few hours) to reduce post-Christmas stress.

3. Prepare the person with dementia for the family gathering

Preparing your loved one for the upcoming events can allow both of you to enjoy the warmth of the season.

- Talk about and show photos of family members and friends who will be visiting.
- Have a 'quiet' room in case things get too hectic.
- Play familiar music and serve favourite traditional Christmas foods.
- Schedule naps, especially if the person usually takes naps.

4. Prepare family members and friends

Preparing families and friends by giving an honest appraisal of the person's condition can help avoid uncomfortable or harmful situations.

- Familiarise family members and friends with behaviours and condition changes.
- Recommend practical and useful gifts (see Tip 7).
- Remind family and friends of the best way to communicate with a person with dementia (see Tip 6).

5. Involve everyone when selecting activities

Involve everyone in activities, including the person with dementia.

- Consider taking walks, icing cakes, telling stories, doing chores, making a memory book or family tree, or keeping a journal.
- To encourage conversation, place magazines, scrapbooks or photo albums in reach; play music to prompt dancing or other kinds of exercise.
- Encourage young family members to participate in simple and familiar activities with the person.

6. Communicate with success

Dementia can diminish a person's ability to communicate. These tips may help you understand each other.

- Be calm and supportive if the person has trouble communicating.
- Speak slowly with a relaxed tone.
- Avoid criticism. For example, when someone forgets a recent conversation, avoid saying, 'Don't you remember?'
- Address the person by name.
- Be patient, flexible, and do not argue with the person with dementia.

7. Intelligent gift giving

- Encourage family and friends to give useful, practical gifts for the person such as comfortable, easy-to-remove clothing, CDs of favourite music, DVDs and photo albums.
- Advise others not to give gifts such as dangerous tools or instruments, utensils, challenging board games, complicated electronic equipment or pets.
- If possible, involve the person in giving gifts. For example, someone who once enjoyed cooking may enjoy baking; or buy the gift and allow the person to wrap it.

8. Safe environment in the home

People with dementia may experience changes in judgement. This behaviour may lead to confusion, frustration or walking around a great deal. Consider these tips to reduce the risk of injury and situations that could be confusing to someone with dementia.

- Assign a 'friend' to watch out for the person to ensure his or her comfort.
- Arrange ample space for walking side-by-side, for wheelchairs and walkers. Keep walking areas clear.
- Consider seating options so the person with dementia can best focus on conversation and be least distracted.
- Don't serve alcohol, which may lead to inappropriate behaviour or complications with medications.

- Accommodate changes in vision. Place contrasting-colour rugs in front of doors or steps. Avoid dark-coloured rugs that may appear to be holes.
- Limit access to places where injuries occur, such as a kitchen or stairwell. Check temperature of water and food. Prevent falls by installing metal grab bars; and secure textured stickers to slippery surfaces.
- Create an even level of lighting; avoid blinking lights.
- Keep decorations simple; avoid using sweets, artificial fruits/ vegetables or other edibles as decorations.
- Supervise taking of medicine.
- Keep emergency phone numbers and a list of medications handy.

9. Travel wisely

The following suggestions may ensure a positive travelling experience:

- Never leave the person alone.
- Use familiar modes of transportation and avoid peak travel times.
- Keep plans simple and maintain daily routines as much as possible.
- Allow extra time to avoid the stress of rushing.
- Advise service and hospitality staff that you are travelling with someone with dementia and about the person's behaviours and special needs.
- Arrange for services such as wheelchairs ahead of time.
- Provide identification items such as a contact numbers that the person may carry in a handbag or wallet. Ensure that clothes are labelled or easily identified as belonging to the person.

10. Reliable sources of support

It is helpful for families to have a list of local resources at hand in case of necessity, for example, GP number, NHS Direct. Staff will answer questions about warning signs of distress in people living with dementia and will wish to assist them and their caregivers.

An A–Z of Scripture promises to support you on your journey

Ask and you will receive.

Be not afraid, I go before you always.

Christ yesterday, today and for ever.

Do not be afraid, for I have redeemed you.
I have called you by your name, you are mine.

Every day, every hour, every moment has been blessed by the touch of his love.

Think of the Flowers growing in the fields: they never have to work or spin, your heavenly Father feeds them.

Live by the Gospel: Matthew, Mark, Luke, John.

How Happy are the poor in spirit; theirs is the kingdom of heaven.

Love one another as I have loved you.

Do not Judge and you will not be judged

Be Kind.

Lord, you examine me and you know me.

Mary, mother of Christ.

Nowhere have I seen faith like this.

Do unto Others as you would have them do unto you.

Peace I leave to you; my peace I give you.

Jesus put this **Q**uestion to His disciples:
'Who do people say that I am?'

Reap a harvest of good works.

You are on a **S**acred journey.

Trust

Lord of the **U**niverse

Victorious Lamb of God

All **W**isdom is from the Lord and it is his own for ever.

I have given you an e**X**ample so that you may copy
what I have done to you.

My soul **Y**earns for you, my God.

As with **Z** we complete our alphabet, may we remember
that you are the Alpha and the Omega.

Books and activity materials

Sonas Training – Communication skills, etc. www.sonasaPc.ie

Speechmark publications – www.speechmark.net or available from booksellers including Amazon – market a range of CDs, games, books and audiobooks that can revive memories. These include the CDs **Sounds Nostalgic: Radio Theme Tunes from the 40s & 50s** and **Sounds Nostalgic: Voices from the 40s & 50s**; a set of cards, **Famous Faces: talking and Remembering**; and **Treasured Memories**, a board game.

It's Still Me, Lord, a DVD highlighting the Spiritual Care needs of people with dementia. Available from:
The Catholic Trust for England and Wales
39 Eccleston Square
London SW1V IBX
020 7630 8220

Dementia: Walking, Not Wandering. Mary Marshall and Kate Allan. Hawker Publications. ISBN 978-1-87479-068-6

Contented Dementia. Oliver James. Vermilion Publications, London. ISBN 978-0-09-190181-3

Losing Clive to Younger Onset Dementia. Helen Beaumont. Jessica Kingsley Publishers. ISBN 978-1-84310-480-3

Ethical Issues in Dementia Care. Julian C. Hughes and Clive Baldwin. Jessica Kingsley Publishers. ISBN 978-1-84310-357-8

Dancing with Dementia. Christine Bryden. Jessica Kingsley Publishers. ISBN 978-1-84310-332-5

Going Against the Stream: Ethical Aspects of Ageing and Care. Peter Jeffrey. CSSP Gracewing Publishers.
ISBN 978-0-85244-541-9

Dementia Reconsidered. Tom Kitwood. Open University Press
ISBN 978-0-33519-855-9

Hearing the Voice of People with Dementia. Malcolm Goldsmith. Jessica Kingsley Publishers. ISBN 978-1-85302-406-1

Dementia and Social Inclusion. Anthea Innes, Carole Archibald and Charlie Murphy. Jessica Kingsley Publishers.
ISBN 978-1-84310-174-1

A Guide to the Spiritual Dimension of Care for People with Alzheimer's Disease and Related Dementia: More than Body, Brain and Breath. Eileen Shamy. Jessica Kingsley Publishers.
ISBN 978-1-84310-129-1

I'm Still Here. John Zeisel. Avery.
ISBN 978-0-74995-221-1

The Alzheimer's Society (www.alzheimers.org.uk) publishes a series of books by David Sheard titled **Being, Enabling, Nurturing, Inspiring** and **Growing**. Also available in a pack of five as **Feelings Matter Most**.

Useful organisations

Alzheimer's Society
Devon House
58 St Katharine's Way
London E1W 1LB

020 7423 3500
0845 300 0336 (helpline open 8.30am – 6.30pm weekdays)

enquiries@alzheimers.org.uk (general information)
www.alzheimers.org.uk

The UK's leading care and research charity for people with dementia and those who care for them. The helpline provides information, support, guidance and referrals to other appropriate organisations.

Alzheimer's Society Talking Point

http://forum.alzheimers.org.uk/

Online discussion board run by the Alzheimer's Society for carers to exchange messages with others who may be in a similar situation.

Admiral Nurses
Specialist mental health nurses supporting people with dementia and their families.

0845 257 9406

direct@dementiauk.org
www.dementiauk.org/what-we-do/admiral-nurses/

British Institute of Learning Disabilities
Campion House
Green Street
Kidderminster DY10 1JL

01562 723 010

enquiries@bild.org.uk
www.bild.org.uk

Body that works to improve the lives of people with disabilities. Provides a range of published and online information.

CJD Support Network
PO Box 346
Market Drayton TF9 4WN

01630 673 993 (admin)
01630 673 973 (helpline)

info@cjdsupport.net
www.cjdsupport.net

Supports people with prion diseases, including forms of Creutzfeldt-Jakob disease (CJD). Provides a range of information on the various forms of prion disease, and works with professionals to improve the level of care provided for people with these conditions.

Harmony House Dementia Support Project
Baden Powell Close
Off Goresbrook Road
Dagenham
Essex RM9 6XN

0208 526 8200

siobhansshjm@aol.com
or srsiobhan@harmonyhousedagenham.org.uk

A community-based project to support younger people with early onset dementia and their families. Pastoral support and training available on request.

Dementia Care Matters Ltd
29 Bloomsbury Place
Brighton
East Sussex BN2 1DB

01273 242 335

info@dementiacarematters.com

An independent team specialising in working with organisations and their staff in developing Dementia Care Services and Mental Health Services for Older People.

Huntington's Disease Association
Neurosupport Centre
Norton Street
Liverpool L3 8LR

0151 298 3298

info@hda.org.uk
www.hda.org.uk

Association that provides information, advice, support and useful publications for families affected by Huntington's disease in England and Wales. It can put you in touch with a regional adviser and your nearest branch or support group.

Multiple Sclerosis Society
MS National Centre
372 Edgware Road
London NW2 6ND

0808 800 8000 (free helpline, weekdays 9am – 9pm)

helpline@mssociety.org.uk
www.mssociety.org.uk

Charity providing information and support to anyone affected by MS. Has a national helpline and a network of over 350 local branches.

National Association of Providers of Activity for Older People (NAPA)
Bondway Commercial Centre
Unit 5.12, 5th Floor
71 Bondway
London SW8 1SQ

020 7078 9375

info@napa-activities.co.uk
www.napa-activities.co.uk

Voluntary organisation dedicated to increasing the profile and understanding of the activity needs for older people.

Niemann-Pick Disease Group (UK)
11 Greenwood Close
The Pastures
Fatfield
Washington NE38 8LR

0191 415 0693

niemann-pick@zetnet.co.uk
www.niemannpick.org.uk

Not-for-profit organisation that supports and promotes research to find a cure or treatments for all types of Niemann-Pick Disease and provides support services to individuals and families affected.

Parkinson's Disease Society of the UK
215 Vauxhall Bridge Road
London SW1V 1EJ

0808 800 0303 (helpline 9.30am – 5.30pmn)

hello@parkinsons.org.uk
www.parkinsons.org.uk

Charity that provides information, advice and support and helpful publications for people with Parkinson's disease. It can put you in touch with your nearest branch, offering information, support and social contact for people with Parkinson's and their families.

Pick's Disease Support Group

0845 458 3208

frontotemp@aol.com
www.pdsg.org.uk

Supports people with fronto-temporal dementia and other forms of dementia, including alcohol-related brain impairment. Provides information and advice, publishes a range of booklets, and has a network of local contacts. Also supports professionals involved in the care of people with these forms of dementia. Organised on a regional basis – check website for local contacts.

Young Dementia UK (formerly The Clive Project)
PO Box 315
Witney
Oxfordshire OX28 IZN

01993 776 295

email@youngdementiauk.org
www.youngdementiauk.org

Works with younger people with dementia and their families in the Oxfordshire area.

Help and information for drivers

Drivers Medical Group
DVLA
Swansea SA99 1TU

0300 790 6806 (Monday to Thursday 8am – 8.30pm,
Friday and Saturday 8am – 5.30pm)

eftd@dvla.gsi.gov.uk
www.dvla.gov.uk / medical.aspx

Driving assessment centres

NORTH ENGLAND

Wrightington Mobility Centre
Wrightington Hospital
Hall Lane
Appley Bridge
Wigan WN6 9EP

01257 256 409

North East Drive Mobility
Walkergate Park
Centre for Neuro-rehabilitation and Neuro-psychiatry
Benfield Road
Newcastle upon Tyne NE6 4QD

0191 287 5090

William Merritt Disabled Living Centre and Mobility Service
St Mary's Hospital
Green Hill Road
Armley
Leeds LS12 3QE

0113 305 5288

MIDLANDS

Derby DriveAbility
Kingsway Hospital
Kingsway
Derby DE22 3LZ

01332 371 929

Regional Driving Assessment Centre
Unit 11, Network Park
Duddeston Mill Road, Saltley
Birmingham B8 1AU

0845 337 1540

EAST ENGLAND

East Anglian DriveAbility
2 Napier Place
Thetford
Norfolk IP24 3RL

01842 753 029

Hertfordshire Action on Disability Mobility Centre (HAD)
The Woodside Centre
The Commons
Welwyn Garden City
Hertfordshire AL7 4DD

01707 324 581

SOUTH/SOUTH-EAST ENGLAND

South East DriveAbility
Cobtree Ward
Preston Hall Hospital
London Road
Aylesford
Kent ME20 7NJ

01622 795 719

Queen Elizabeth's Foundation Mobility Centre
Damson Way
Fountain Drive
Carshalton
Surrey SM5 4NR

020 8770 1151

WEST/SOUTH-WEST ENGLAND

Mobility Service Living (dlc)
Vassall Centre
Gill Avenue
Fishponds
Bristol BS16 2QQ

0117 965 9353

Cornwall Mobility Centre
Tehidy House
Royal Cornwall Hospital
Truro
Cornwall TR1 3LJ

01872 254 920

WALES

South Wales Mobility and Driving Assessment Service
South Wales Disability Resources Centre
Rookwood Hospital
Fairwater Road
Llandaff
Cardiff CF5 2YN

029 2055 5130

North Wales Mobility and Driving Assessment Service
Disability Resources Centre
Glan Clwyd Hospital
Bodelwyddan
Denbighshire LL18 5UJ

01745 584 858

NORTHERN IRELAND

Northern Ireland Forum Centre
Disability Action
Portside Business Park
189 Airport Road
Belfast BT3 9ED

028 9029 7880

SCOTLAND

Scottish Driving Assessment Service
Astley Ainslie Hospital
133 Grange Loan
Edinburgh EH9 2HL

0131 537 9192